Take
aways

a LITTLE BOOK
of
REFLECTIONS

Susan Winters-Griste

Cover and Text Design by StickyEarth.com

First Paperback Edition

ISBN 978-1530567645

Printed in the United States of America

TO ALL MY "TEACHERS", PAST AND
PRESENT, WHO HAVE SHARED
THEIR WISDOM WITH ME.

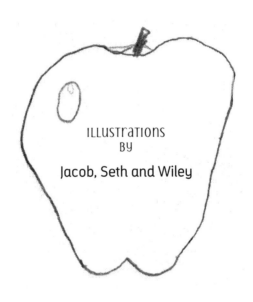

ILLUSTRATIONS
BY

Jacob, Seth and Wiley

∿

Table of Contents

Acknowledgements

I hope to extend deep gratitude to Maria G. for her amazing gift of editing and to Melody Templeton for the guidance and support in bringing this project to life. I am thankful to my parents for their presence and unfailing love. I especially recognize Annette Murray with her creativity and Mrs. Watson and Barbara S. who shared their loving touch as this neared completion. Lastly, but definitely not least, I give thanks to the men in my life: Jacob, Seth and Wiley, who offered their illustrations that complement the ideas of this little book.

TAKE
AWAY

DEFINITION:

"a key fact, point or idea to be remembered, typically one emerging from a discussion or meeting"
(Oxford Dictionaries)

All is Well

When considering our life journeys and the moments we encounter, how do we notice when "All is Well"? For some of us, it may be when the children are all tucked away in their beds. For others, it may be when we are sitting around the table sharing a favorite meal with our loved ones. Or maybe it's after a long week entering the weekend toward freedom from the "clock." Still others may experience "All is Well" when soul meets soul in a healthy communication exchange.

How do you experience "All is Well" moments on your journey? How can you create more of them?

Hooks and Anchors

Hooks – those inconvenient situations in which we find ourselves under the power of an event or a person or a circumstance, which "reel" us into a "reaction" rather than a "response."

Anchors – thoughts, mantras, ways of being that ground and steady us to allow for a thoughtful response.

All of us encounter "hooks" on our journey that can trigger us to react from a place of fear, anxiety or anger rather than with the freedom to respond out of our wisdom. It is important to be aware of our "hooks" and to move toward our "anchors."

What are "anchors" for you? What seems to be a grounding force in your life?

THree

Our Classrooms

Are you imagining rows of desks? A chalkboard in front of you? Students with notebooks and pencils ready to write and learn? That is often the image I retrieve, yet along the way I have recently discovered that my image of classroom has expanded a bit. I now find that the teachers in my "classroom" walk the planet and appear in my life in more mysterious ways. In fact, it seems my "classrooms" and teachers come alive as soon as I feel challenged, puzzled, disoriented and most noticeably, when agitated. These life lessons compel me to look inward and respond from a place of calm. The chalkboard heading becomes the "art of expressing emotions" rather than reacting solely on them.

 What life experiences have become your classroom moments?

Temperature Check

Life has a way of getting away from us with the unceasing busy schedules we find ourselves living. This can lead to "automatic pilot" living and a difficulty in maintaining an awareness of where we are on this journey. In my training, I learned a helpful tool called a "Temperature Check" that can allow for a self-check or "life read" moment. When practiced, it can be illuminating and give us a sense of perspective.

*Complete the following sentences
to take your temperature:*
I wish...
I feel...
I need...
I realize that I...

*Dig deep and uncover what
your heart may be saying to you.*

Lighthouses

Can you picture it? A beautiful, tall and magnificent structure majestically standing on the coastal ground of "salvation"? When we consider the sacredness of the lighthouse mission and the countless lives saved by the radiant light, we might ponder what sacred encounters in our life bring a sense of illumination and light to help us to navigate the dark or foggy trials in our days.

When facing dark moments, what do you notice as helpful in adding "light" to a situation?

Is This a Crisis or an Inconvenience?

Crisis – "time of great danger or trouble, whose outcome decides whether possible bad consequences will follow."

Inconvenience – "not favorable to one's comfort, difficult to do, use or get to."

Is it fair to say that we all know and recognize that life can be difficult and has its challenges? Yes, the statement that "stress is a part of life" rings true for every creature on this planet.

When stress is upon us, it can be difficult to maintain perspective on the situation. I have found that asking the question: "Is this a crisis or an inconvenience?" brings me to a clearer vision of the matter at hand. Once we have established the level of urgency, we are more present and better empowered to respond with an appropriate action.

Considering these definitions, what are you aware of that may once have been considered a crisis but now may truly be an "inconvenience"?

IF YOU BREAK YOUR NECK, IF YOU HAVE NOTHING TO EAT, IF YOUR HOUSE IS ON FIRE, THEN YOU GOT A PROBLEM. EVERYTHING ELSE IS INCONVENIENCE.

Robert Fulghum

Negativity Bias

Are you familiar with the term "Negativity Bias"?
We have the "fortune" of inheriting from our ancestors (think pre-historic cavemen and cavewomen) a tendency and inclination to seek out the negative aspects of life and to register them in our psyche more dominantly than the positive.

Why?
Because it was those humans who were more prone to anxiety, worry and fear that survived and lived to pass on their genes. Those human beings who were carefree or "happy-go-lucky" were eaten or killed by the saber-toothed tiger.

So how does this matter today in the 21st Century?
Well, scientists have found the Negativity Bias ratio is 3:1, which means that for every negative experience, we actually need three positive experiences to counteract it.

A thought to consider:
Consider the following examples, when practiced consistently we increase the reward chemical in our brain called dopamine. This can result in a more optimistic perspective and reinforce our brain's seeking out more things to be grateful for.

Examples: Gratitude Journals, Appreciation Meditations, Taking in the Good

 How might you begin to incorporate positive practices into your life?

ONCE YOU REPLACE NEGATIVE THOUGHTS WITH POSITIVE ONES, YOU'LL START HAVING POSITIVE RESULTS.

Willie Nelson

Language as Instrument

What language do you speak? No, I am not referring to native tongue or language of origin. Actually, I am asking what attention you bring to the language and words that you use to communicate. Are your words too often harsh like a clanging symbol or do your words express a soft and soothing melody in delivery of your message?

The importance of words and the manner of their expression is often overlooked. The occasions in which communication is strained are often related to poor word usage. Consider a piano with all of its keys and the way one note is played with another, we can parallel how we select our words to share with another.

 Are there any communication patterns that you would like to "tune up" by choosing a more melodic approach to your wording?

Graveyards

How often do we pass cemeteries in our travels and not pay any mind? I, too, was untouched by any instance of driving past graveyards, big or small. Over the years, and as life has ticked on, I have come to experience cemeteries as holy ground. When pondering all the past lives that are at rest in those special plots of soil, one can reflect on life at present and cherish our precious time on this earth.

Visiting a graveyard can be a profound experience when the speed of life overwhelms us. Visiting a cemetery brings a certain "pause" as life is so still when standing on the holy ground. I find I feel more alive when I am standing on such holy ground, such that it actually becomes life giving ground for me.

In the next week, find time to visit a graveyard, spend a few moments and notice......how do you experience this sort of "pause"?

Breeze and Gusts

A light breeze can feel refreshing and comforting on a warm summer day. The light tingle on your skin may be a welcome touch from Mother Nature. Wind gusts, however, are a different experience and sensation. Most of us would prefer that they cease. Gusts of wind can often take our breath away, as well as many of our precious objects.

In contrasting the breezes and the gusts of life, how do we experience each? Do we offer gratitude for those "breezes" that cool us down after an intense encounter? As far as "gusts" in life, how do we bear down within and remain steady? Envision in your mind a great oak tree. Its branches may sway in a strong gust, yet it is otherwise unmoved.

As you look within, what are you aware of that instills steadiness, calm and strength?

Four-Letter Words

No, not those kinds....silly!

Rather I am asking you to focus on the four letter words that bring more of a sense of peace and tranquility into your life.

Do any of these four-letter words resonate with you?

LOVE, CALM, HOPE, EASE, REST, LIFE, GOOD

 What may be some of your own "four-letter" words?

THE WORLD IS DIVIDED INTO
TWO CLASSES. THOSE WHO
BELIEVE THE INCREDIBLE AND
THOSE WHO DO THE IMPROBABLE.

Oscar Wilde

Wishes, Hopes, and Dreams

Sure, when we were younger we did our share of dreaming of what life would be like when we grew up. Yet, even as adults, there is still room for wishes, hopes and dreams as we continue to move forward in our journeys.

Can we all consider that continued wishing, hoping and dreaming allows for us to move along in "growing up"? Is it conceivable that when we cease wishing, hoping and dreaming, we cease to develop and grow up?

What are you wishing, hoping and dreaming for today?

A Slow Dance

Can I have this dance? A waltz would be lovely!
In our world today it seems that most of us are in
a fast dance/quick step movement. Faster and
faster it seems the feet and brains need to work.
I prefer a slow rhythm; an image of an elderly
couple dancing to a slow melody with light and
airy movement comes to mind.

*If you translate this to your own
daily living, what might your
"dance" look like?*

LET YOUR LIFE LIGHTLY DANCE
ON THE EDGES OF TIME LIKE
DEW ON THE TIP OF A LEAF.

Rabindranath Tagore

Sounds

There are noises in our lives. Do we pause to notice what sounds of comfort we most cherish? For example, I welcome the sound of my teapot boiling (as loud as it can be). I relish the "notice" that my teatime is near! I also adore the lovely sounds of wind chimes outside my window. They bring such sweet melodies to my ears. The sound of my sons' laughter from down the hall always brings a smile to my face.

What "sounds of comfort" do you most treasure and enjoy?

Gratitude is Golden

Gratitude: "a feeling of appreciation or thanks."

Would you like to add a sparkle of cheer to your days? You might consider beginning a practice of offering gratitude moments to those 24 hours we meet upon each day. It is often helpful to choose a specific time of day and a number from one to ten of gratitudes to meditate on for that day.

Are there two people in whom you are especially grateful in your life? What is it about them for which you are grateful?

SIXTEEN

Goodwill

A translation — to will goodness toward others. Narcissism and self absorption seems to run rampant in our society. Yet, we can often find those individuals who exude a sense of "good will" and kindness in their demeanor and actions. I recall moments (maybe small gestures but of huge significance to person receiving) of good will in action:

— A shopper who corrected a cashier who gave too much change

— An individual who gave up his or her seat on train for another

— A person in line at a coffee shop who paid for the next ten customers in line

Can you remember a situation in which you witnessed good-will in action? How do you feel when recalling the experience?

EVERY INDIVIDUAL HAS A PLACE
TO FILL IN THE WORLD, AND IS
IMPORTANT, IN SOME RESPECT,
WHETHER HE CHOOSES TO BE
SO OR NOT.

Nathaniel Hawthorne

Roles We Hold

Mother, daughter, father, son, wife, husband, aunt, citizen, neighbor, nurse, caretaker, etc. It can be fascinating to contemplate the myriad of roles we hold in life, each one with its own special contribution or experience. I invite you to consider the roles you maintain. It may strike you that we bring different parts of ourselves to the various roles that we live out.

Is there a certain role that you have found to be more fulfilling and satisfying? Why do you think that is so?

WHEN WE REMEMBER WE
ARE ALL MAD, THE MYSTERIES
DISAPPEAR AND LIFE STANDS
EXPLAINED.

Mark Twain

Mystery

Each of us has encountered those mind-boggling moments, baffling situations and difficult individuals that tug at us to no end. These can create in us an unstoppable itch to figure out and answer the question "why". Often we discover the answer or solution. However, occasionally we are left in unceasing puzzlement and perplexity. In these situations, it is helpful to announce, "I surrender, you are a mystery to me." I find that when wrestling leads to more confusion and distress, it may be time to surrender to the mystery.

Take Away   Is there a person or circumstance currently leaving you perplexed or puzzled? Can you experience greater peace by surrendering to the mystery?

Solitude

As our world has become increasingly "plugged in" and we have become wired to our devices, we seldom experience the true solitude that we may have known in the past. This three-syllable noun can have such a profound influence on our well-being when practiced in appropriate moderation. Although we are designed to be in relationship, the practice of creating moments of solitude can be helpful to allow for reflection, contemplation and overall intrapersonal discovery without distraction.

Are you comfortable with solitude? Why or why not? How can you become more comfortable and allow for greater reflection?

Twenty

Invitations

Most of us love to receive invitations to weddings, birthdays, graduations, picnics, etc., and look forward to wonderful opportunities to gather with our friends and families to celebrate. We can also have many living encounters that invite us to pay attention to certain approaches or ways of moving in life.

We recognize "Living Invitations" as those thoughts that circle back in our minds and seem to tug at us to get our attention. We may even notice, "there is that thought again".

If we go a bit deeper and ask about our "Living Invitations," we might consider how our lives are inviting us to live more fully. Am I being asked to be of service in a certain area?

Have you noticed a whisper asking you to listen more closely....is it an invitation to try something new?

Twenty-one

U-Turns

How do you manage life when you recognize that it's time to turn around? Do you complain, curse and stomp your feet in frustration? Or do you express thanks for the insight that led you to realize that it is time for change or a course correction? To be honest, I have done the former, and at times will catch myself slipping back into old patterns of thinking. Over the last few years, I have made it an intention to pay attention to how I respond to changes, false starts and misguided choices. Now the mental steps I take are:

1 - place foot on break

2 - turn wheel

3 - redirect.

What steps do you take when you are in the stage of making of a U-Turn?

Miracle Question

If while you sleep tonight, a miracle happens, what would you be doing differently? I love this question! Can you guess the key word in this question? Yep, it's YOU! So often many of us think "if this person or that situation were different, then the problem would be solved".... and sometimes that is accurate. However, more often than not, it is the changes in ourselves that make all the difference.

How would you answer the Miracle Question?

Response or Reaction?

Most of us are aware that we have triggers that set off a negative emotional experience. Some of us are triggered by a person who cuts us off in traffic, by dirty dishes left in sink, by children continuing to whine for the same thing over and over, or by nosy co-workers gabbing on the latest gossip.

At these times, before we give power over to the emotions, it is important to pause and consider: "Will this statement be a response or a reaction?" What is the difference, you ask?

Reaction is simply an intense automatic output of emotion with little or no attention given to how the reaction will be received. In contrast, a response, after brief pause, registers emotion and thoughtfully considers how to share a particular emotion. We have power when we pause to respond.

In what situations would you like to move toward a Response rather than a Reaction?

Dogs as Mentors

What do you see when you look into your furry friend's eyes? I see complete and total unconditional love.

These furry friends truly behave as if we are the world's greatest creation. The loyalty and friendship they embody provides us with a model to strive for. I have a plaque at home that reads: "Be the kind of person your dog thinks you are."

What kind of person would you like to be? What decisions can you make today to move toward that goal?

Twenty-Five

Heroines and Heroes

It seems lately the SuperHero films have stolen the show as they rise to record breaking levels of sales, viewers, and popularity. Ironman, Superman, Batman, Captain America, Wonder Woman... have mega screen time and have impacted many a young child's mind.

As adults when we contemplate who are (or who have been) heroes and heroines to us, what individuals come to mind? Is it a neighbor who saw your patio furniture blowing over and came to the rescue to secure it in place? Is it a teacher who noticed your child's sadness and gave him a special poem to offer cheer? Is it a co-worker who offered to take on another task so you would be able to leave early for vacation?

Take Away

Are there more local heroes you can think of to emulate?

TWENTY-SIX

Be Still and Know Calm

Life has a way of bringing difficulties to our paths and it may feel like we are on a ship in the midst of a severe storm at sea, being tossed about endlessly. So how in the world can we be still when such tempests are raging upon us?

One practice that is simple, yet so powerful is to remember to focus on the breath. When we close our eyes and bring attention to the breath, we calm the mind and spirit. Try it... close your eyes, inhale and feel the air filling your lungs. Now exhale and feel your stomach fall and relax. Stay with this movement for about 30 seconds and notice how you feel afterward.

Take two deep breaths, focusing on the word "calm". How do you feel?

TWENTY-SEVEN

Self-Care

Care of self. How is that going for you? I know in my life it has been rather elusive and I know that much of the responsibility for that is my own. Self-care is a necessity. We all have our share of excuses, reasons why we do not seem to make it a priority in our lives. None of them is good enough to allow our self-care to suffer.

Consider the image of a flower that regularly needs water to grow and thrive. We, too, need nurturing in order to grow and be in good health. Let's agree to become gardeners tending to our own well-being.

How will you choose to provide yourself with some form of self-care? Today? This week?

TWENTY-EIGHT

Clarity

It is a wonderful experience to have clarity of thought and mind. Often times, however, we feel as though cobwebs have entered our minds. Sometimes "sleeping on it" or journaling can be helpful. Once the fog has lifted, we find ourselves more in touch with our inner awareness. We then can move into, and operate from our wiser selves.

Do you have a strategy in place for when those foggy moments happen?

Presence – Levels of Being Present

Have you often wondered about how others perceive you? I am not referring to their opinions of you, but rather, how they experience you in your "presence."

By presence, I mean how you look, how you sound, or how you come across when expressing your thoughts. You may also consider how you convey your authentic self and how your energy is translated.

Whom have you encountered recently that brings a "sense of presence"?

Humor

It's true! Humor and laughter really are great forms of medicine. Laughter releases endorphins in the body similar to the effects of a physical workout that stimulates the feel-good chemicals in the brain. Researchers have demonstrated that laughter raises our ability to tolerate discomfort. When we are able to laugh and not take life too seriously, we can provide our own intravenous dose of cheer while also increasing the positive effects on our body.

How can you bring more humor into your life?

Compliments

It is great to receive a compliment! More importantly, you can effect a powerful movement when you give them. A suggestion: make a commitment to offer five sincere compliments per day. They need not be to the same person. Compliment different people — spread the cheer.

What was the last compliment you gave today? What made the action you are complimenting praiseworthy?

Whistle While You Work

Work takes many different shapes and forms: like chores, going to an office, gardening, moving, driving, cooking, etc. Some of us may find enjoyment from what others may consider "work." When a task before me requires more of my energy, I have found it helpful to begin whistling a tune of some sort. Consider the words from the song, from the 1937 animated Disney Film, Snow White and the Seven Dwarfs, "Whistle While You Work":

> *"Whistle while you work and cheerfully together we can tidy up this place. So hum a merry tune, it won't take long when there's a song that will help you set the pace. When hearts are high, the time will fly, so whistle while you work."*

 When in your daily life would whistling be a helpful practice?

AMONG THE SEVERAL KINDS
OF BEAUTY, THE EYE TAKES
MOST DELIGHT IN COLORS.

Joseph Addison

Colors

Do you have a favorite color? Mine happens to be purple. I just love the shade of purple that you find each year in the Spring's hyacinths. When you think about your favorite color, what shade is most enjoyable to you? Close your eyes and visualize that shade for a moment. Now, when you have one of those gloomy days, try a "color meditation." Close your eyes, take a deep breath, and imagine your favorite color and some scenes or objects that include that color. Stay with image for about 30 seconds and then take another deep breath. Continue this meditation for about two more repetitions.

 What is your favorite color? What attracts you to that particular color?

THIRTY-FOUR

Tugging Calls

Have you ever experienced a tugging at your spirit, but you could not quite discern what the cause of the tugging was? Similarly, you may have sensed at times that something was not quite right, but had difficulty figuring out what that "something" was. When these moments happen in our lives, it is helpful to:

1. Have patience around the experience (urgency often leads to more confusion);

2. Seek out quiet and silent space;

3. Ask your Spirit within for clarity and wisdom in discovering the root and message of the "tugging calls."

How have you moved through the experience of "something seems off"?

Questions

Some of us believe that asking questions could make us look stupid or unintelligent. I am a firm believer in the adage that there are no stupid questions. In fact, it is in the questions that we ask ourselves, in particular, that leads us to a deeper wisdom. Recently, a few of my questions are: How have I been witnessing to my thoughts this week? What am I preoccupied with that influences my choices? What am I craving?

 What questions are you asking yourself today? This week?

I STRIVE FOR THE BEST AND
DO THE POSSIBLE.

Lyndon Johnson

THIRTY-SIX

Chutes and Ladders

Have you ever played the Milton Bradley game "Chutes and Ladders"? If you have, you would recall the happiness felt when landing on a space that had a ladder and allowed you to climb ahead in the game, as well as recall the discouragement experienced when the slide space resulted in slipping all the way down the board. As adults we are well aware that life is not a complete upward movement. We know that life will include downhill moments which may be uncomfortable to tolerate. On acknowledging the reality of the ebb and flow in life, we may find it useful to examine how we move into each one.

Getting in touch with your adult self and paralleling to set-backs and climbing the proverbial ladder, how do you encounter each?

THE VALUE OF A REALLY
GREAT STUDENT TO THE
COUNTRY IS EQUAL TO
HALF A DOZEN GRAIN
ELEVATORS OR A NEW
TRANSCONTINENTAL
RAILWAY.

William Osler

Word Study

One of the subjects my 11 year old son has in school is called Word-Study. In a nutshell, it is what we used to call Spelling in our grammar school days. The term Word-Study compels me to reflect on words which I would like to study. Consequently, I became acquainted with new words that hold much meaning and depth:

Integrity   Love

Gratitude   Compassion

What words would you like to study?

GREAT MEN ARE THEY
WHO SEE THAT SPIRITUAL
IS STRONGER THAN ANY
MATERIAL FORCE, THAT
THOUGHTS RULE THE WORLD.

Ralph Waldo Emerson

Thinking Powers and Stress

When I work with children, I often utilize the term
"thinking powers" to refer to ideas and solutions
for particular situations the youngsters are
struggling to handle. I give the child I am working
with a small notebook and we mark down each
"thinking power" that he or she will work on until
our next meeting. We share techniques like deep
breaths to help ourselves calm down, butterfly
hugs to comfort ourselves if nervous, and also
happy thought practices, if we're sad or angry.
As grown-ups, we acknowledge that stress,
difficult emotions and challenging relationships
are parts of life. Each of us may have our own
message we use to reduce the effects of stress.

*What "thinking powers" do you use that
help navigate stressful situations with
more ease?*

Easy Does It

Take it easy....what does this catch phrase mean to you? For me, I think of small steps, taking things a little bit at a time. It is amazing how just iterating words like easy, small, steps, little, and bits can melt away stress.

What terms do you consider that soften a difficult experience?

MOST PEOPLE WOULD SUCCEED IN SMALL THINGS IF THEY WERE NOT TROUBLED WITH GREAT AMBITIONS.

Henry Wadsworth Longfellow

Sons and Daughters

Children, whether young children or adult children, are still our sons and daughters. They are our beloved, extensions of our hearts, living and breathing on this earth. Our sons and daughters are our most precious and treasured souls walking this journey with us. Beyond genetics and DNA, there is such a connection to this other human being that is profoundly felt in the depths of our psyche. We adore our children and can recognize the miracle of life every moment we gaze into their eyes.

When you look into your child's eyes, what do you see?

"Escapes"
Healthy Options

Yes, there are times when the world feels like a bit more than we can handle. On those occasions, finding "refuge" to regroup and disengage may be a helpful option. What are your "escapes"?

Some of my escapes are going to see a good movie, baking cookies, reading a good book, slipping in a family video, or listening to instrumental music. These are just a few examples of some ways to take time to reenergize.

Take Away *Have you found your "escape" to be of a healthy nature? Are there any "escapes" that you recognize as unhealthy? Are there ways you can transform them into a healthy "escape"?*

I Spy...

Are you familiar with the children's book series, "I Spy," by Walter Wick and Jean Marzollo? Over the years, my son and I have worked through several of the books and enjoy the challenge of finding hidden objects.

In life, I have found it pleasing and fun to seek out those hidden moments of joy each day. Some examples that may be readily observed, but easily overlooked:

A clean glass window

The twinkling of a small star

A swing blowing in breeze

The loving gaze of a friendly dog

A small bird perched on a wire

A street lamp glow

 What do you consider "spy worthy"?

On Loss

In living life, we do not often have the idea of loss on our minds. In fact, I believe we do our best to keep it at a distance. When we do encounter loss, how do we move through the journey? Some of us go within, others seek out support and solace from circles around them. There is not one "right" way of healing after loss, only a "way" that is best for you. You may not know it, though, until after you have lived through it.

What have you noticed about yourself when you encounter loss?

Messages

Communication can be such a "tricky" business. Often what we intend to say does not necessarily come across to the receiver as we had intended it to. That is why it is so important to reflect back the message we heard to clarify if we understood it correctly.

Some of the most useful reflections are: "Did I hear that correctly?"; "I heard you say....is that right?"; "Tell me more so I understand completely your message."

 How do you manage the situation when someone misinterprets your message?

Numbers

What is your favorite number? Do you recall how it became your favorite number? Numbers are all around us. The amazing reality of numbers provides us with directions, recipes, dates of the year, checks and balances, weather reports, and countless other forms of information. It is difficult to imagine life without numbers! Numbers can absolutely be a helpful part of life or not....Are there occasions when numbers become the dictator of how we live? For some of us, it is how many friends we have "following us" or how many awards we received or how much money we make that can impact how we make our choices.

Are numbers a "part" of your life or do they lead you?

Self-Expression

Yes, there are many ways to express yourself. Some express self through music, art, tattoos, fashion, etc. In day-to-day conversation, what can be observed in how we express ourselves with others? Do we come from a place of calm? From a place of sarcasm? Skepticism? Love or anger?

Take Away *When expressing self, what is your ideal way of communicating? Can it be improved by coming from a place of calm and love?*

A MAN'S CHARACTER MAY BE
LEARNED FROM THE ADJECTIVES
WHICH HE HABITUALLY USES
IN CONVERATION.

Mark Twain

Forty-seven

Act As If

For those of us who desire to grow in a certain area of life, it is often helpful to live by the template "act as if you have courage, strength, generosity, etc., though you have it not." In practicing the "fake it till you make it" approach, you may find you can develop a quality by "acting as if" you already have it.

Is there an area of your life that you could begin "pretending" is true until it becomes so?

Just Because

I was once at a convenience store for coffee and when it came my turn in line, the cashier stated: "No charge." I surprisingly asked, "Why?" The kind cashier said that a few minutes earlier, a gentleman paid for the next ten shoppers' coffee purchases and preferred to be anonymous. After I returned to my car, I took a moment to consider this generous man's gesture and wondered what inspired him to choose today. We are often driven to act, move, and decide because of a purpose. Conversely, are there moments when you recognize there may not necessarily be a purpose or reason for an action but you go ahead anyway — just because?

When you move into a "just because" moment, how do you celebrate it?

Love Barriers

To love is to live life fully. Yet, for many of us, there are barriers or blocks that get in the way of us feeling free to love. Some of the blockades are anger, resentment, hurt, or vulnerability. Some think that these are good reasons to withhold love and often remain in a state of distance and disconnect. Others may recognize that there is a figurative wall around them that serves to protect them from potential further hurt. Nonetheless, they choose to risk letting down their wall in an effort to love and stay true to their authentic selves in living life fully.

Are there any barriers preventing you from fully living and loving that you can decide to heal and let go?

"Poisons"
What Are Yours?

Yes, we are all aware and familiar with the elements in nature and scientific formulas that are poisonous or toxic. When we consider behaviors, choices, and encounters in life, do we recognize which have a "poisonous" effect on us? For some, it may be a dead end job, for others a one-sided friendship and for others it could even be an abusive relationship.

What do you recognize as toxic or poisonous in your life journey?

FREEDOM OF SPEECH AND
FREEDOM OF ACTION ARE
MEANINGLESS WITHOUT
FREEDOM TO THINK.

Bergen Evans

Free and Clear

Often we feel burdened or weighed down by the many responsibilities and challenges of life. How do we move toward experiencing a "free spirit" despite the realities and difficulties in life? By "free spirit" living, I am referring to how we find a clear vision of encountering challenges with a sense of freedom to choose our attitude.

What situations in your life would you like to approach with a "free and clear" attitude?

Gentle Touch

Many of us, especially those of us with Type A personalities, are driven to excel, and often have perfectionistic natures. Those of us who have acquired such traits often find it difficult to be gentle and soft in our treatment of ourselves. It is important for us to learn how to "parent oneself" with a gentle touch. Consider the "young child within".....what kind of treatment does he or she deserve?

How might you treat yourself with a kinder and gentler touch?

FIFTY-THree

Ebenezer Scrooge

Most of us have read or seen the classic Charles Dickens' novel, A Christmas Carol. The infamous character of Ebenezer Scrooge moves into a conversional experience. He sheds the skin of a previous way of living and after three visits from the "Spirits," he begins to transform and create a new way of living life. Have you recently or in the past felt the sense of a conversional experience? For us, it could be a decision to give up smoking which brings a healthier approach to life. Or, it could even be a choice to remove critical and negative language and begin to utilize more positive and uplifting statements.

Take Away *Have you experienced a conversional movement in your life? In what ways have you moved into a new way of living? Were you able to maintain your new posture? If not, can you regain it?*

FIFTY-FOUR

Imprints

Imprint – "to implant firmly in the mind or to fix in the memory, a lasting effect or characteristic result."

We all have particular memories or experiences that have left their "mark" on us either physically or emotionally. Many have become significant indicators of how we live out our lives. For many of us, an imprint could be the loss of a parent, spouse, or child. For others of us, we may have been considerably impacted by our high school years or after our first romantic relationship.

After some reflection, what stands out in your mind as a formational moment that shaped how you approach life?

Hunger Pains

The growling stomach, lightheadedness or a lack of energy often alert us that we need to be fed. Physiologically, it is a basic need. When we think of a hungry spirit, there are different alerts that tell us our spirit needs to be fed. We are often signaled by increased fatigue, irritability, anxiety or feeling unhappy. For some of us, our spirits are fed by music, art, books, meditation, prayer, etc. The most important aspect to consider is for us to pay attention to our "hunger pains" and not neglect our spirit.

What tells you that your spirit is hungry? For what does your spirit hunger?

FIFTY-SIX

On Love

Many have attempted to define it, write about it, find it, keep it (hold onto it), abuse it, manipulate it, and quench it. I find the most fascinating aspect on love is: "How do I live out love so as to share love in all encounters?" It is important to remember that love is not only a feeling but also a verb. Love, in action, can change lives.

*How do you most
demonstrate love
in action?*

LOVE IS ENERGY OF LIFE.

Robert Browning

Who, What, Where?

There is a fun and entertaining game created by University Games called "Who, What, Where." It involves a player sketching a who, a what and a where and the other players guess the scene being described or represented in the drawing. After I last played the game, I found myself asking bigger questions related to who, what and where. I began asking random questions about my life, questions such as:

Who do I choose to surround myself with?
What do I enjoy? Where do I find peace?

How would you ask and complete the questions beginning with:
Who do I....
What do I.....
Where do I...

Chaos

When we encounter chaos, do we absorb the effects and over-identify with the situation, thereby allowing the chaos to dictate our choices? It is important for us to be attentive to our recognition of "self" as separate from the situation. Then we have a stronger ability to draw from our inner strength of "Being" to make choices in a non-chaotic manner.

 When do you most often experience a sense of chaos? Are there choices that you can make that could decrease the chaos?

Cruise Control

Many of us have moments "when it rains, it pours." Often just getting one foot in front of the other is the success for the day. We may need to make an inventory of priorities and allow some items to fall under "cruise control." We know it is important to still drive and take the wheel, yet for the present time, we can only manage maintaining the same settings. Once additional energy resurfaces then we can make adjustments.

 What "setting" are you on at the present time? What aspects of your life fall under "cruise control" right now?

Wounds

As human beings, we have physical and emotional vulnerabilities. Physically, after an injury, we can often still see a scar after the injury itself has healed. When we consider emotional wounds experienced in our history, it is obviously far more difficult to see the resulting scars. Many emotional wounds run deep and leave psychological scars that surface and re-open, often sub-consciously. These inner wounds are more difficult to heal as they are not readily observed. It is important for us to give as much care to our psychological scars as we would to our physical injuries and pain.

Do you know scars from your past that re-open when facing certain encounters? How do you tend to those scars?

Power Struggles

Power – "great ability to do, act, or affect strongly; vigor, force, strength."

How can we recognize and determine if we are heading into a "power struggle"? Power struggles surface when we begin to lose our sense of being and enter a competition of control as to whose voice is heard and who is considered "right," versus who is "wrong." This frequently destroys any movement toward understanding and compromise.

 Take Away

Are you noticing any power struggle at this time in your life? What could you do differently that may interrupt it?

Options

We live in a world that indulges us with multiple choices for beverages, food, sizes, and colors. Although we enjoy the variety and selections, have we been conditioned to always expect more? Does that leave us continually in a state of discontent?

 At what times do you feel it is important to say "Enough!"?

Jammed Up

I once met an individual who had a peculiar saying for when she felt stuck. She often would make the statement: "I'm jammed up like a big old copy machine." For most of us when dealing with a frustrating copy machine, steps we take are usually: stop, open all the drawers, check all the paper and push re-set. When paralleling to moments in life when we feel stuck or "jammed up" in our thoughts, we may find it helpful to develop a sequence of steps to aid us in sorting through our multitude of thoughts.

Take Away *How do you manage that feeling of being stuck, confused or uncertain? What sequence of steps could you practice that could allow for clearing the "jam"?*

We're Off to the Races

Is there a person in your life with whom you often clash? For those of us who are pulled in and find we have lost our cool, it may seem we are off and running to see who comes out the winner. Difficult as it may be, it is important for us to maintain our sense of calm and to know that in certain circumstances we should "never leave the gate." Then we may discover a dance of healthy communication, rather than a race bound to end with no real winner.

What strategies in your life can you employ to prevent you from "leaving the gate"?

Our Senses

The wonder of our senses can be profoundly experienced when we reflect on our amazing faculties. To smell a pot of chicken noodle soup on the stove is extraordinary when we allow ourselves to stop for a moment and breathe that in. To hear the beautiful sound of our church choir singing "Amazing Grace" can touch our souls. To see the gorgeous sunset on a spring evening can bring us to a state of awe.

Take Away *What smells leave you most grateful for having a nose that can smell? What sights make you most grateful for having two eyes that can see? What sounds are you most grateful about having two ears that can hear?*

ALL CREDIBILITY, ALL GOOD CONSCIENCE, ALL EVIDENCE OF TRUTH COME ONLY FROM THE SENSES.

Friedrich Nietzsche

Essentials

Things that one person thinks as necessary for living may be totally different from someone else's ideas of essentials. I am not referring to our basic needs, but more of our created ideals in terms of lifestyle. Some may consider essentials to include: perfume; athletics; owning a pet; having a garden; education, etc.

 What have you defined as "essentials" in your life?

SIXTY-SEVEN

Windows and Walls

What do you like most about windows? I most appreciate windows as a pathway to the outdoors and a step closer to nature when you need to be indoors. I also find windows to be a much more pleasant accent than a wall. Walls divide us. Windows allow in.

When in your life are there times for windows and when are times for walls?

Birthdays

Date of Birth: Not telling

As we age and annually experience another birthday, we add another year to our lives. We also add another filing cabinet of memories. I know many of us are more inclined to be of the anti-aging posture, considering the discomforts of aging on the body. I won't lie, that part can be uncomfortable. However, I like to think of another birthday as another year of new wisdom gained to live more fully until the next birthday.

How do you encounter your Birthday each year?

Attractive

I am going to make an assumption that most of us go right to idea of appearance...tall, dark and handsome or blond, thin and beautiful? Yet, when we ask what makes a person attractive, do we consider qualities, disposition, talents, and creativity? Next time, might we ask what captures attractiveness as a human being?

What do you consider as "attractive" in a person?

Journaling: Me, Myself and I

Journaling has often been a very helpful practice for individuals in collecting thoughts, expressing innermost feelings and as an instrument of reflections. I have often found that an inner dialogue with "Me, Myself and I" sets me onto a pathway leading toward my own clarity and wisdom. The internal conversation with the different parts of myself written out in my journal has allowed for a narration of concerns, feelings, or questions. This gathering of "Me, Myself and I" brings a fully present self and opens a door to an awakened perspective.

Have you discovered any awakenings through journaling?

Come, Sit Down

Yes, we are all "on the go" on what may seem like the never ending "treadmill of life." For those non-stop functioners, it is very important for us to listen to that voice inside us that beckons us to "come and sit down for a while."

Take Away *How often do you pay attention to the voice within asking you to come, sit down and rest for a little while? What prevents you from listening?*

HE THAT CAN TAKE REST
IS GREATER THAN HE THAT
CAN TAKE CITIES.

Benjamin Franklin

One Chair and a Book

For me, that's my formula for a pleasurable and comfortable afternoon. For others, it may be ten wings and two beers, for others one bike and a backpack, or two sneakers and a road.

What is your formula for a few pleasurable hours?

A FORMULA IS SOMETHING THAT WORKED ONCE, AND KEEPS TRYING TO DO IT AGAIN.

Henry S. Haskins

Family

Families come in all shapes and sizes. When we think of family, most of us think of our blood kin. For many of us, however, "family" extends beyond our blood kin. We may have been blessed with unique friendships that through the course of time have certainly deserved the title of "my family." Whether blood ties or friendship bonds, each has their own expression of connection.

When meditating on the word "family", who comes to mind? What defines family for you?

The Norm

Our lives have a way of falling into a pattern or routine. We wake up, get dressed, go to work, drop kids off at school and move into our day. For some of us, we may experience a sense of monotony. We seek less of a prosaic arrangement and more of a diversified schedule. Others of us take comfort in the daily order of operations.

How do you experience the "norm" in your life?

Let It Go

Have you had a bad day? Did you make a mistake or mess up a project? Did you strike out? If you answered yes to any of the questions, I would like to take a moment and welcome you to the club. On these occasions that may bring stress, if your first thought is one of "gloom and doom" you are beginning a stress reaction. You can minimize your stress reaction by turning difficult situations around and taking control of your response. Take a deep breath in, and then fully breathe out the experience in your exhale and repeat: "I am choosing to let it go."

Think of how you handled challenging situations in the past, what seemed to be helpful actions? What seemed to create more stress?

Candles In The Room

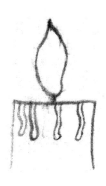

I love staring at a candle's flame! Have you ever tried it...taking a few moments and looking at the flicker of candlelight? When I consider my own flame within, I reflect on how to maintain a glow, but it is also important to be mindful of what may cause that flame to dim. In knowledge of what may dim your light, you may then be more prepared to learn ways to prevent such an occurrence.

How do you keep your candle lit and bring light into a room?

Steeples

More recently, I have found my eyes drawn toward steeples when they fall within my range of sight. Even while driving, I have noticed my gaze lingering a little longer on the tall structure in the distance. I often take a second glance and think about the sacredness of the building it accents. For me, steeples have been an invitation to remember what is sacred and to give thanks for all the blessings of life.

When you happen upon a steeple, what comes to mind for you?

Valuables

We all have experienced a moment when we realized we had taken something for granted, maybe a job, a car, a person, or even a washer and dryer. Often it is after something is broken, lost or gone that we realize how valuable it is to us.

What holds value to you? Have you realized something was valuable after it was gone? What was it?

TRUE FRIENDSHIP IS LIKE
SOUND HEALTH: THE
VALUE OF IT IS SELDOM
KNOWN UNTIL IT IS LOST.

Charles Caleb Colton

Five Steps to Clarity

Step 1 – Take a deep breath

Step 2 – Take a helicopter view, rising above yourself in your mind

Step 3 – Notice what you feel

Step 4 – Emphasize in statement, "I am not that feeling, my body is feeling _____, but I am separate from my feeling."

Step 5 – Ask yourself, what are my feelings asking me to pay attention to?

In separating self from feelings, how could this be helpful in your life?

Train Tracks

When I drive over railroad tracks, I often think about all the trains, freight cars, tankers, that have passed this way and wonder where have they been and where are they going. A word that comes to mind is journeys. Those steel and wooden beams were laid down to allow for a journey.

 What has been laid down for your journey?

Let's Eat

Family meals are so precious, especially in these busy days when it is so difficult to have everyone at the table at once. On those occasions when we do have the fortune of sitting down all together, my favorite words are "let's eat!" When we eat together, we have the opportunity to share in one another's presence and experience a sense of gathering.

What are favorite words you have that express a movement toward gathering?

THE WORST SIN TOWARD
OUR FELLOW CREATURES
IS NOT TO HATE THEM,
BUT TO BE INDIFFERENT
TO THEM: THAT IS THE
ESSENCE OF INHUMANITY.

George Bernard Shaw

Let's Go to the Zoo

Most of us have been to a zoo at some point in our lives. Have you been to one lately? It is so amazing to ponder all the many creatures on this planet. Consider the King of the jungle—the lion, the elephant . . . and numerous other living admirable wonders of nature and acknowledge the remarkable fact: We too, are fellow creatures on this planet.

 Is there a particular animal or creature that brings you a sense of "living wonder"?

Sense of Self

Many of us believe self-esteem is built externally....our achievements, awards, accomplishments, credentials, titles, etc. To consider the alternative that self-esteem is created from within requires a shift in thinking. To dig deep and have a conviction to say "I know who I am for my own sake," versus "I know what I have done," can lead to a life altering experience allowing you to rejoice in yourself.

In what ways do you rejoice in who you are, as opposed to what you have done?

Achilles' Heel Lessons Taught

Most likely we are familiar with the Greek Hero, Achilles, whose whole body was immune to pain except for his heel, which was not immersed by the magical water of the River Styx. Today we use the term "Achilles' Heel" to refer to an individual's weakness. When we consider our own "Achilles' Heel" in life, what can it teach us about how we face vulnerability?

What do you consider to be an "Achilles' Heel" in your life?

Signs to Live By

Road signs are common visuals when driving
or riding along road. From Yield to Stop, to

, you get the
idea. For me, the words on the sign that say
SLOW DOWN hit home on a regular basis.
I am beginning to listen and make an effort
to live out the directive of this sign.

*On contemplation, what road
sign best captures your sense
of journey at moment?*

Sirens in the Distance

The word "siren" comes from Greek mythology as a term that describes a sea creature that lured sailors in by their singing and to what ultimately would be their demise. Today we think of sirens as alerting us to danger or warning of threats nearby. When hearing those sounds in the distance, do we wonder who is in need? Next time we hear a siren in the distance, reminding us of our humanity, may we send out thoughts of care and concern.

What thought or prayer could be offered up next time you hear a siren?

Caregivers

Most of us recognize those in the traditional roles of caregiver: parents, adult children of aging parents, nurses, doctors, etc. When we really think about this term as "givers of care," are we not all in this role?

Can we give "care" when we hold a door open for someone else?

Can we give "care" when we offer our place in line to a mother with little children?

Can we give "care" when we mow the lawn of our elderly neighbor?

Can we give "care" when we see the sadness in a widower's eyes as he mourns the loss of wife?

 How might you "give care" this week?

Mountain Climbers

I have climbed several mountains in my life and have a few still to scale. No, they were not Everest or the Alps, rather my mountains  were more symbolic representations of my journey. A few of the "mountains" I have climbed are called Patience, Fear, Depression and one that I am still climbing – Balance.

 What mountains have you climbed?

LIFE AFFORDS NO HIGHER PLEASURE THAN THAT OF SURMOUNTING DIFFICULTIES.

Samuel Johnson

Hand Over Heart

When we notice our emotions simmering and realize we are becoming overwhelmed, a possible movement for self that often brings a calming effect is to place a hand over our heart and remind ourself to "Be still and breathe deeply."

Take a moment, place your hand over your heart. Fully inhale and exhale, and recite, "Be still and breathe deeply," while feeling your heartbeat.

How do you see this practice being of comfort to your journey?

Lukewarm

Do you sometimes experience in your encounters an unsure or half-hearted tepid assessment? Often we do not have enough information to know if we are pro or con, positive or negative on a subject. Once we gather more information, we gain a stronger sense of where we stand.

Sometimes, however, despite all the information, we may find ourselves lukewarm on a person, position, or statement. When that occurs, we may feel very uncomfortable with our uncertainty and indecision.

When feeling "lukewarm" how do you tolerate the uncertainty? How do you constructively try to move to a place of certainty?

Can You Feel It?

There is an old Jackson 5 song called "Can You
Feel It?" On hearing this tune more recently,
I considered not so much the lyrics, but the
question of "Can you feel it?". For me "it" led to
a consideration of life. Can you feel "Life"? Is it
through the heart pumping in your chest? Is it in
the air that flows in and out from your nose? Is it
through your eyes when you observe elements in
nature bearing witness to life?

How do you feel a sense of living?
When do you feel most alive?

Letters

When was the last time you wrote a letter? No, I am not referring to notecards, texts, or emails, but rather a thoughtful hand-written letter. Some of us may have experienced pen-pal writing when younger or writing of a letter to a loved one who had been in the service. I recall enjoying in the "old days" receiving letters in college from friends and family who extended their cheer letting me know they were thinking of me. I imagine you, too, can remember an instance where you received a letter and it made your day or brought a smile to your face.

In the present day, is there anyone you have been thinking about who may appreciate the thoughtful expression that comes with writing a letter?

Joy
Rejoice and Be Glad

What comes to mind when you think of individuals with a joyful spirit? I have encountered many folks throughout my life and travels who certainly would be described as joyful. They seem to have a glow about them, a twinkle in their eye and a lightheartedness that is naturally gravitating. Being of good cheer and sharing this movement with others can be a conversional experience for both ourselves and those individuals we encounter.

Consider, what is one way you can bring joy to others in your life?

Rest Rooms
Room for Rest

We have come to know the Restroom as spaces for, well, "taking care of business." When thinking about the term in two separate words: Rest & Room, how can we allow for room in our lives to rest? We have so many busy rooms and "to-do" rooms, that for many of us, it leaves little room to stop, breathe and rest.

How do you allow room for rest in your life? What spaces are occupied that prevent you from giving your soul time to rest?

Keys

Keys open locked doors, cabinets, chests, etc. Keys are known for opening what is locked or closed. Turn the key and the car comes to life and the journey begins. Keys to one's heart and soul enter another realm of living. For many individuals, kindness, love, and gentleness are what open their hearts. For others, it is when they experience a deep intimacy with another human being. Others may finally open their hearts when they have moved through a profound forgiveness of self after a long experience of shame or guilt.

What are keys that open your heart? What unlocks the gate to your soul?

Coping Styles

As we live through life and face stressors along the way, we often develop a certain way of dealing with stress that becomes a patterned way of coping. Some of us seek out comfort and others of us avoid or minimize the situation. Even further, some of us may even become destructive as a release of stress toward ourselves or others. Think about your coping style, how do you typically manage a stressful situation?

 How has your coping style influenced the ways you live through stress?

Thinking Twice

Believe it or not, we all talk to ourselves silently every day. This mental conversation is considered self-talk. Sometimes during these mental conversations we turn a minor fault or problem into a big one. These "messages" often replay themselves in our heads leading us to have negative cognitions. It is often our self-talk that determines how we will respond to situations.

There is a helpful technique called the "thinking twice motto" which emphasizes that we all have "first thoughts" but can think again. An example of the "thinking twice motto" follows on the next page.

Situation: Presenting to a large audience

First Thought: "I will never be able to speak in front of all those people."

Second Thought: "I will be sure to prepare and practice well before my presentation. If I make a mistake, I will learn from it."

In changing the message to a positive one, over time, our minds can more likely play out these new and positive messages. This helps us to more confidently manage challenging encounters.

In what situations do you think it would be helpful to "think twice" or have a "second thought" ?

Word definitions found throughout *Take Aways*
are sourced from the following:

Merriam-Webster Dictionary

Oxford Dictionary

Webster's New World Dictionary